To Sue,

Find Your
Buried Treasure

Treasure every day!

Betty Liedtke

Find Your Buried Treasure

Nuggets Mined from Everyday Life

Betty Liedtke

The columns in *Find Your Buried Treasure* were originally published in the *Chanhassen Villager* and are being reprinted with permission of the *Chanhassen Villager*. Some of the columns have been edited slightly since they were first published.

Published by FuzionPress, 1210 E 115th Street, Burnsville, MN, USA

Cover Design & Interior Book Design: FuzionPress

Library of Congress Control Number: 2016944392
ISBN: 978-0-9974938-0-1

Dedication

This book is dedicated to my family, friends, neighbors, and the many total strangers who have inspired me through their words and actions. Thank you for helping me see the treasures that are all around us in our everyday lives.

A Note from the Author

March 1, 2001. That's the day my life-long dream of becoming a newspaper columnist came true, with my first column published in the *Chanhassen (MN) Villager*. A few weeks later, Unsie Zuege, a features reporter for the paper and also a good friend, said to me, "You know what I love about your column, Betty? In every one, there's a nugget—something of value for the reader to take away."

My first thought was, "What a nice thing for her to say." My second thought was, "What the heck is she talking about?"

I went back and read over the columns that had already been published, looking for nuggets, and I found them—life lessons learned and shared, and simple words of insight and inspiration.

That's been my guiding light ever since.

Never once, however, in the 15 years I've been writing for the *Villager,* have I ever sat down at my computer, rubbed my hands together, and said, "Okay, what's this week's nugget going to be?" I don't think about "nuggets" at all as I'm writing each column. I just know that by the time I'm done there had better be one. Otherwise I'm just rambling, and nobody wants to read that.

Some of my greatest satisfaction comes from the comments and email I regularly receive from people saying that something I've written has made a difference in their lives. They tell me they've been inspired or influenced in some way, or they've changed their attitude or actions because of something they read in my column. I enjoy knowing they found a nugget that they, too, could hold on to and treasure.

Even so, I've always had trouble answering a question people often ask when they find out I'm a newspaper columnist:

"What do you write about, Betty?"

I usually find myself stammering or struggling for words until I come out with something like, "Oh, just everyday things. Insights and observations on day-to-day life."

Not exactly an inspiring or engaging response, and it certainly doesn't do justice to the wisdom and wonder that can, indeed, be found in everyday life.

From time to time, I also get asked, "When are you going to publish your columns in a book?" Actually, I *have* started, on several different occasions, to put together a collection of some of my columns, all centered on a particular theme, like "My All-Time Favorites," or columns about family, holidays, or my attempts to get organized once and for all.

None of these efforts ever got off the ground, however. It always felt like something was missing, but I could never figure out what it was, or why it was so elusive.

Finally, though, I realized what was missing, and what needed to be at the core of any collection I put together: nuggets.

I went back through the roughly 800 columns I've written over the years. I was looking for those that had a powerful or profound—yet easy-to-find and easy-to-grasp—nugget. I wanted to find the columns that had especially meaningful words of wisdom, advice, or inspiration that would be relevant to virtually anyone, no matter what their age, gender, or station in life.

I ended up with thirty columns—two from each of the years I've been writing for the *Villager*. Following each column, I added a suggestion for ways in which readers could look for similar or related nuggets in their own lives instead of just reading about mine, because I've come to realize over the years that valuable treasures and delightful discoveries are, indeed, all around us, even in our everyday lives. *Especially* in our everyday lives. However, we have to be looking for them, or at least paying attention when we come across them. Otherwise, they'll slip right by us without our even noticing them. Or they'll just lie there, buried and dormant, not doing us or anyone else any good.

That's how this book came to be.

If you're a regular reader of my column, either in the *Chanhassen Villager* or on my blog (www.findyourburiedtreasure.com/blog)—thank you! I hope you'll enjoy this collection as a stroll down Memory Lane, or perhaps as a way to catch some of the columns you might have missed the first time around.

And if this is all brand new to you, welcome! I hope that reading about some of the nuggets of wisdom and inspiration I've found in my own life will help you see all those that are in yours—so that you, too, can find yourself with a treasure chest full of wisdom, inspiration, insight, and adventure that will enrich your own life, and those with whom you choose to share it.

Table of Contents

Chapter 1 - March 1, 2001

Old Movie, New View

The *Wizard of Oz* has always been my favorite movie. I'm not sure why. Maybe it's the songs, or the scenery, or even those cute little Munchkins—especially the ballerinas and the ones with the lollipop.

Perhaps it's just the familiarity of it all. In the days before fast-forward and pause buttons, *The Wizard of Oz* was on TV every year in the spring, usually around Easter. Our family would gather 'round the television set and settle in for the evening with a big bowl of popcorn made the old-fashioned way, before anyone had microwave ovens.

Today, I enjoy the movie just as much as I did years ago, but for different reasons. As Dorothy dances down the yellow brick road trying to find her way back to Kansas, I find myself more interested in the underlying theme of the movie than in flying monkeys and houses.

The view is different now from the other side of the rainbow, partly because I see things differently as an adult than I did as a child, and partly because the world has changed so much since then. Families today are hard-pressed to find time enough to sit down to dinner together, let alone to find a spot on the calendar when everyone can be in the same place at the same time long enough to gather around the television set and watch a movie straight through in one sitting.

Mostly, though, I think everything looks so different because I'm the mom now. Much as I hate to admit it, I can identify a lot more with Auntie Em than I can with the girl in the ruby slippers and the blue-checked dress.

When my kids leave for school in the morning, I usually don't worry that they'll be carried off by a tornado before they can get back home safely. But a whirlwind of other dangers is waiting to snatch them away if given half a chance—and there are plenty of temptations for excitement and adventures that they can't find in their own back yard.

As a parent, I walk a fine line every day between trying to protect my children from the world and giving them the freedom to explore it, and between encouraging them to be curious and teaching them to be cautious. I also try to overlook the fact that when Dorothy was pondering the mysteries of the world while balancing herself on a railing, she slipped and landed in a pigsty.

I guess one of my jobs as a parent is to try to provide a soft landing for my kids in case they fall. I hope I'm doing that, and they'll grow up knowing that our home is a safe haven to which they can always return.

I can't shield my children from all the problems they'll have to face in life. I know they'll constantly be confronted by wicked witches, strange surroundings, and unmarked intersections that don't give them a clue as to which road to follow. I also know, and I hope they'll remember, the lesson that Dorothy finally learned by the time she made it to the Emerald City.

Maybe that's the real reason I love the movie so much—because Dorothy was right after all. There's no place like home.

 There's no place like home. But the view is different now, because we see things differently as adults than we did as children, and because the world has changed so much since then.

Find Another Nugget: What was your favorite movie as a child? Why? Locate a copy of it and watch it now. Notice whatever new or different perspectives you have from watching it as an adult.

Chapter 2 - August 9, 2001

The Pretzel Pose

For a long time now, I've been thinking about taking a yoga class, even after playing a trivia game in which yoga was the correct answer to the question, "In what type of exercise do you stand on your head?"

The reason I've been thinking about it for so long, as opposed to actually doing it, isn't because I was lazy or procrastinating. It's because I was scared. Not about the standing-on-my-head part, although that's not something I've ever put on my "Things I Want to Do Today" list. What terrified me was the lotus position.

I think the lotus position is the universal yoga pose. I also think "the pretzel position" would be a more accurate name for it. It's the pose in which a person sits, relaxed and reflective, with eyes closed, hands placed comfortably on the knees, and each foot resting gently on the upper thigh of the opposite leg.

That doesn't work for me.

The way I figure it, if God wanted my feet and thighs to be that close to each other, he wouldn't have put the femur—the longest bone in the body—between them.

Still, I know a number of people who swear by yoga. Last year, while on vacation at the beach, I met a woman who was thin, blonde, tan, and gorgeous. Generally, I try to stay away from people like that, but she was friendly, too, and we chatted for a few minutes every time we ran into each other. At one point, she mentioned that she recently lost the sixty pounds she had gained during a painful divorce and difficult custody battle. She credited her weight loss to yoga.

"It's all in the breathing," she said. Never once did she mention lotuses—or pretzels.

A close friend of mine, who recently started taking a yoga class, said that even after just one or two classes, she could feel the difference in her strength and flexibility. Last week, another friend told me that when his mental and physical states were at an all-time low a number of years ago, yoga literally saved his life.

So I finally signed up.

The first thing we did in class was to lie on our exercise mats in a quiet room with the lights off—relaxing, aligning our spines, and concentrating on our breathing. The second thing we did, at least the second thing *I* did, was try not to fall asleep. Then we were led through a series of poses with interesting names, like dying swan, downward dog, and modified cobra. Animals figure very prominently in yoga.

By the time we were finished, I did feel relaxed and refreshed, although I wasn't tan, blonde, or sixty pounds lighter. I know I had a good workout because I was sore the next day, the way you're supposed to feel when you wake up and shake up muscles you haven't used in a while. I expected to feel it in my back and my legs, but I also felt it in my fingers, my ankles, and my dying swan.

Throughout the class, the instructor kept reminding us not to push, pull, or stretch past our comfort level, and not to do anything that hurts. Still, she encouraged us with each move to work just a little harder, and to reach just a little farther.

It suddenly occurred to me that that's how you get results in yoga class or in anything else. Push, pull, and stretch. Work a little harder, and reach a little farther, but don't do anything that hurts.

I think I'm going to adopt this as my personal philosophy. I also think I'll continue going to yoga class, and set some goals for myself along the way. One of them will be to keep pushing, pulling, and stretching until I can actually get into the lotus position.

And I won't stop there. I'll keep practicing until it's so easy I can do it standing on my head.

 To achieve success in anything, you need to push, pull, and stretch. Work a little harder, and reach a little farther, but don't do anything that hurts.

Find Another Nugget: Attend a class, seminar, workshop, presentation, or demonstration on a topic that's new to you. Even better is if it's something you've been curious about or have wanted to check out or do "someday." Now's the time!

Chapter 3 - April 11, 2002

Your Assignment

I'm warning you right up front that this week's column is going to involve homework. So if you're not up for it, you can stop reading right now.

It's not a very difficult assignment. It involves spending a few minutes with some people you trust, and who know you well. Immediate family is ideal, but a small group of good friends will work, too. If you really want to have a great experience, try it both ways.

Here's what you do. Grab a pen and some paper. Gather your "team" together. Then ask them to tell you your positive traits, including all the things they like about you. Give them a few minutes to think about it before you start. While each of them is talking, make no comments. Just write down everything they say.

There's no time limit, no quota, and no magic word that someone has to guess before the buzzer goes off. You can be done in three minutes or you can take all evening, especially if you decide to take turns and do the same for everyone in the group.

The important rule for the people giving the comments is to remember that everything must be completely positive. No hidden meanings are allowed, no "constructive" criticism, no insults disguised as compliments. They can't say, "You'd be absolutely beautiful if you changed your hairstyle," or "I love how you looked when you were ten pounds thinner," or "Your meatloaf tastes a whole lot better than that enchilada thing."

The person receiving the comments must simply accept them. This can be a hard thing to do. Many of us, especially women, don't have the slightest idea what to do with a compliment when we get one. If someone says, "You really did a nice job!" we answer, "Well, I had a lot of help," or, "I just got lucky." If people say they like the sweater we're wearing, we respond, "Oh, this is so old." We reject and deflect compliments instead of simply accepting and appreciating them, and we never hear what people are really saying: "You're a hard worker." "You have good taste." "You are talented." "You've got style."

I had to do this exercise recently as part of a group project. I did it with my family, and again with a group of close friends. In both cases it was scary and intimidating, but also enlightening. It's comforting to be told, out loud, that we are valued and appreciated. It's heartwarming to hear, in specific detail, the positive traits others see in us—even if we had to ask them to tell us what they are.

Actually, asking is the hardest part of this whole exercise, which is why I'm giving it to you as a homework assignment. You're probably not comfortable going up to someone, even someone you love and who loves you, and saying, "Tell me all the things you like about me." So instead, tell them it's an assignment, and you have to do it.

Then do it.

Officially, the purpose of this exercise is to show you your strengths and to help you determine what it is you truly want in life, but I found that it does a whole lot more.

It gives you a healthy dose of self-esteem and self-confidence, which is always nice to receive—whether you're a quart low or you already have a full tank. It polishes your personality and shows you the areas in which you shine. It gives the people who care about you an opportunity to tell you why, and it gives you a chance to do the same for them. Mostly, it opens our eyes to the good in ourselves, and in the people who mean the most to us.

So that's the homework. I'd like for you to do it right now. Or this evening, or this weekend, but no later than that.

I'll expect the completed assignments on my desk first thing Monday morning.

 It's comforting and heartwarming to be told, out loud, that we are valued and appreciated, and to hear in specific detail the positive traits others see in us.

Find Another Nugget: Put together a short list of people you trust, and who know you well. Ask each of them to tell you your positive traits—all the things they like about you. Make no comment while they're talking, just write down everything they say. The only response necessary when they're done is, "Thank you." After you've talked to everyone, spend some quiet time alone with your list. Take in and enjoy everything that was said about you.

Chapter 4 - June 6, 2002

Laundry Lessons

I had the most wonderful experience the other day. It was interesting, it was inspiring, it was gratifying, and it reaffirmed my faith in humanity.

It happened at the laundromat.

I don't go to the laundromat very often, but we have a few queen-size, high-octane comforters that don't fit in my washing machine, at least not without registering on the Richter Scale. So a few times a year, I gather them up, along with every quarter I can find, and head to the laundromat.

Shortly after I got there, a couple arrived with a pile of laundry large enough to have its own area code. The man helped the woman carry it all in. Then he left, and she set about sorting clothes and measuring detergent.

A little later, the woman went over to the change machine, but it wouldn't take the bill she was trying to insert. It had run out of quarters. A look of desperation appeared on her face.

"I still have a lot of laundry to do, and my husband won't be back for a long time," she said.

I dug into my bag of quarters. I had only a dollar's worth left, but my stuff was almost dry.

"Will this help?" I asked. "It's not much, but—"

"I don't have a dollar I can give you," she said. "All I have is this twenty. Do you have change?"

I didn't. I tried to give her the quarters anyway, but she wouldn't take them. I insisted, although I'm not in the habit of forcing my money on other people. This was a desperate woman, however, and a buck wasn't going to bankrupt my retirement account.

She started rummaging through her purse and pockets, and eventually found a dollar's worth of dimes and nickels. So we were even.

By now my dryers had stopped, but one of the comforters was still a little damp. I dug around in my purse until I found another quarter, which was fortunate because I didn't want to have to buy one back from the other lady.

And then I asked her for a favor.

"I have to run to the grocery store," I told her. "Could you keep an eye on my dryer until I get back?"

She was more than happy to oblige, but then she had a favor of her own.

"Could you get me some quarters?"

She handed me her twenty-dollar bill, and I left.

As I was driving to the grocery store, it occurred to me how unusual it was for someone to hand twenty dollars to a perfect stranger, especially one who was on her way out the door. I wondered if I should have at least introduced myself, or left her some collateral, like the magazine I was reading. Then I realized she already had some collateral—my comforter. It was worth more than twenty dollars, but I'm sure that never even occurred to her. Besides, judging from the comforter she was washing, mine didn't fit her style or color scheme.

When I got back, I handed her the rolls of quarters, and picked up my comforter, which was folded neatly on the table.

By the way, I'm pretty sure the woman in the laundromat wasn't born in America. Her accent indicated that she was originally from another country, but that didn't matter to either one of us. There are no language barriers in a laundromat. There are also no religious or cultural conflicts or suspicions. There are only people—armed with detergent, bleach, fabric softener, and quarters.

I left the laundromat that day with more than springtime-fresh comforters. I also took home a few lessons I learned while I was there. For one thing, I learned that it takes three quarters to dry my flowered comforter, but only two for the blue and green one. I also learned that sometimes you have to put your faith in strangers. I learned that trust feels pretty good, no matter which end of the deal you're on.

And I learned that you can meet the nicest people in the laundromat.

Trust feels good, no matter which end of the deal you're on.

Find Another Nugget: Take a chance on someone. Reach out to a stranger, or someone you don't know well. Extend an act of courtesy or a show of faith in some way.

Chapter 5 - January 16, 2003

Listen to This!

I was listening to the sounds of silence recently. Not the song by Simon and Garfunkel, although I like listening to that, too. In fact, whenever it comes on the radio I turn up the volume and sing along on the low part.

But I'm talking about the sounds of silence you hear when you turn off the radio, as well as the television, the computer, the dryer, and the dishwasher. It's not an easy thing to do. In order to really hear silence—which sounds like an oxymoron, but isn't—you have to get as far away as you can from civilization as we know it. The middle of a desert would be far enough. In fact, that's where I heard it.

Over Christmas break, our family took a little post-holiday vacation to San Diego. We visited a lot of different places while we were there, including the zoo, the beach, a museum, a monument, and the desert.

Whenever I hear the word "desert," I think of sand, the Sahara, and movies like *Lawrence of Arabia*. But not all deserts are like that. Some, especially in the United States, offer breathtaking scenery, imposing rock formations, interesting cactus plants, and other unusual vegetation. We stopped our car a few times and got out so we could look around and take some photos. That's when I was struck by the silence—when everyone was perfectly still, when the nearest car was miles away, and when all the creatures of the desert were hidden away someplace where they could be neither seen nor heard.

Now *that's* silence.

There's something very powerful about silence. It forces you to slow down and to use all your senses. When you stop and listen to it, it makes you feel alive and aware in a way you never have before. It reminds me of the old saying, "It was so noisy I couldn't hear myself think." I understand now how true that can be.

I think we could all use a little more silence in our lives. It doesn't need to be the total, absolute kind that you can find only in places like the desert, or the South Pole, or outer space. All we need to do is turn off everything that generates noise and distractions, including that little voice inside us that keeps telling us how busy we are, how much we still have to do today, and what a waste of time this is. Who wants to sit still doing absolutely nothing for five minutes anyway, even if we had five minutes to spare, which we don't, so why does it even matter?

It matters. If you take the time—even for just a few minutes—to sit quietly and listen to the sounds of silence, you'll hear more than you've ever heard before. The hum of the refrigerator. A breeze outside the window. Your own breathing.

Maybe you'll even hear the sound of a car driving down the street a few blocks away—with a Simon and Garfunkel song playing on the radio, and someone singing along on the low part.

> Take the time to sit quietly and listen to the sounds of silence, and you'll hear more than you've ever heard before.

Find Another Nugget: Find the quietest place you can, at the quietest time of the day or night. Close your eyes, and try to empty your mind of any thoughts or distractions, pushing them away when they come back in. Listen to the sounds you usually don't hear or notice—like the hum of the refrigerator, or a quiet breeze. Focus on these as you breathe deeply. After you've spent a few minutes this way, open your eyes, and pay special attention to the thoughts that come to mind before you fully engage back in to your regular activities.

Chapter 6 - June 26, 2003

Family, Friends, and Fruit Salad

"So long," I said to my friend. "Thanks for inviting me to the party. I had a great time."

She just laughed, because the party wasn't actually until the next day, when she would have a house full of people celebrating her daughter's graduation. This afternoon was just for preparation, and several friends and neighbors were helping her slice, dice, chop, and chisel the ingredients for a major fruit salad.

By the time we arrived, cutting boards, knives, paper towels, and zip-top bags were spread out on the kitchen table, along with mounds of apples, strawberries, pineapples, and cantaloupe. After a few jokes about nice melons and about which of us could be trusted with sharp objects, we got down to business. I was in charge of slicing strawberries. As we worked, we continued chatting and joking about our jobs, our families, graduation parties, and anything else that struck our fancy.

"This is how it used to be," I thought to myself. "This is how it *should* be." Pleasant company, easy conversation, quick laughter, and a lot of work that gets done in a short amount of time and doesn't even feel like work.

I come from a large family, so I grew up with that sort of thing. My dad is one of seven brothers and sisters, and I have more than 30 first cousins. Some of them lived within shouting distance of our house, and few of them were more than a fifteen-minute drive away. Every year, there were several communions, confirmations, and graduations in the family, and most of the time we'd have a group celebration for each event. All the moms and aunts would be involved in the planning and preparation, not just the ones whose kids were graduating or being confirmed. And the prep seemed to be as much of a party as the event itself.

The old saying, "Many hands make light work," is true in more ways than one. When many hands are working together, they don't just lighten the load, they lighten the mood. They give people a chance to catch up on family gossip and neighborhood news, and to relax and unwind in mind and spirit, even if their hands are hard at work slicing and dicing, washing and rinsing.

There are plenty of reasons this isn't the normal way of doing things anymore. For one thing, families in general are a lot smaller than they used to be, and they're often spread out across the country, instead of across the street or across town. Most neighbors don't know each other as well as neighbors used to, and they might be less apt to offer or ask for help when it comes to something like preparing for a party or a special event.

But that's a shame. Getting together to get things done is a way of *getting* to know one another a little better, receiving assistance when we need it, and offering assistance when we can. It's a way of connecting, plus it just feels good.

My friend's graduation party went very well, by the way, with plenty of people and a ton of food. All of it was delicious, especially the fruit salad. And if I may say so, the strawberries were sliced to perfection.

 When many hands are working together, they don't just lighten the load, they lighten the mood.

Find Another Nugget: Organize a group activity— one that helps someone accomplish a task or project, but also fosters conversation and camaraderie.

Chapter 7 - January 1, 2004

A Great Opportunity

It was late afternoon on Friday, the week before Christmas. I still had shopping, wrapping, and baking to do. My Christmas cards weren't out yet, and the house needed some serious cleaning. The phone rang. It was one of my neighbors.

"What are you doing tonight?" she asked. "I know this is short notice, and it's right before Christmas and all, but we've got tickets to the Bette Midler concert, and my husband's sick. I was wondering if you'd like to go."

Would I like to go?? To see Bette Midler??

"I'd love to," I told her. "But..."

My mind started racing, thinking of everything I had planned to do that night. Everything I still needed to do, including giving my daughter's friend a ride home from our house later that evening.

"Can I call you right back?" I asked. "I have to check out a few things with my husband."

I hung up the phone, and started to dial my husband's work number. Halfway through it, I stopped and hung up. I looked around the house, at the Christmas cards and wrapping paper on the kitchen table, and the dust bunnies in the corners. I took a deep breath, and then called my neighbor back.

"I really appreciate you thinking of me," I told her. "And if it were any other time of year, I'd drop everything and go."

"I understand completely. I'm kind of wondering myself what we were thinking, making plans like this for right before Christmas."

I thanked her again and hung up just as my daughter was walking into the kitchen. I told her about the neighbor's call, and she shook her head in disbelief.

"Mom, are you nuts? What do you have to do that can't wait until tomorrow?"

I started to reel off my list, and she had a response for everything.

"I can help clean. I can help you bake cookies. I can wrap some presents for you. Well, not mine, of course. And Dad can drive my friend home."

"Go," said my husband when I called him. "Have a great time."

Then I called my neighbor back and asked if the ticket was still available. It was.

I had a fabulous time. The Divine Miss M was as divine as ever. The next morning, when I told my daughter all about the concert, I also thanked her for urging me to go.

"You'd have regretted it forever if you didn't," she said, and I knew she was right. Besides, when I got back to all my chores and projects, it was with quick hands, a light heart, and Bette Midler songs running through my mind.

I'm not planning on making a habit of ignoring and abandoning my duties and responsibilities whenever an opportunity arises. However, I do plan on being more careful not to miss out—as I almost did—on a golden opportunity just because there are other things I need to do. I hope I can always remember that some opportunities do, indeed, knock only once.

Or they call on the phone, late in the afternoon on the Friday before Christmas.

Don't miss out on a golden opportunity just because there are other things you need to do. Some opportunities do, indeed, knock only once.

Find Another Nugget: The next time you hear yourself thinking or saying, "Oh, I'd love to do that, but I can't, because I need to...," take a moment to think of both the benefit and the consequences of doing whatever it is you'd "love to do," and what you "need to do" just then. *Now* make your decision, and act accordingly.

Chapter 8 - December 2, 2004

The Puzzle of Life

People can really be a puzzle. By that I don't mean they're confusing, although they can be that, too, especially if they are teenagers or members of the opposite sex.

What I'm talking about is more like a jigsaw puzzle, where every piece is a little different from every other one, even though they all have the same basic structure. Each piece is as important and necessary as every other one in the puzzle, whether it's an edge piece, a corner, or one of those annoying little wavy pieces that won't stay where it belongs until it's connected to all the other ones around it.

Connecting the pieces is not always easy. Sometimes it's hard even to find two pieces that will fit together. Or it may be difficult to believe that two particular pieces even belong to the same puzzle, because they seem so different from each other. Sometimes you try forcing pieces together that look like they should fit, but don't. Other times you might find pieces that don't look like they belong together, but turn out to be a perfect fit.

People can be like that, too.

A friend of mine brought this up recently, after having a conversation with someone about a mutual friend of theirs. They were discussing how long they had known each other and where they had first met, and my friend used the jigsaw puzzle analogy to point out how people can be connected to each other through a number of other people.

I like that comparison, and not because I've always enjoyed putting jigsaw puzzles together. Instead, I think it's because there's something we could all learn from this if we'd stop to think about it for a minute. It's not really about people or puzzle pieces fitting together. It's not even about finding where we belong in relation to each other. It's simply realizing that we *do* belong, and that we're all part of the same big picture—even if we can't always see it, and even when we don't have any idea how, where, or why we're connected to other people whose looks, beliefs, accents, and politics are so different from our own.

Maybe we should all start thinking of ourselves and each other as pieces of a puzzle—a really *big* puzzle. If we did that, we might be better able to see and remember that every one of us is as valuable as every other. Even though some have more prominent roles, like the corners that anchor the rest of the pieces together, it takes everyone, working side by side and holding on to each other, to put the picture together the way it's supposed to be.

I'm going to try to remember this whenever I come across other pieces of the puzzle that don't seem to fit, or to belong in the same one I'm in. I'll accept that they're simply in a different section of the puzzle, or they make up a different part of the scenery. We may be at opposite ends of the big picture, or a few rows apart. Either way, it's important for all of us to be there.

So maybe people aren't such a puzzle after all. We simply need to figure out how and where we all fit together, or we just need to remember that we do.

Everyone is as valuable as everyone else. Some have more prominent roles, but it takes everyone— working side by side and holding on to each other—to put the picture together the way it's supposed to be.

Find Another Nugget: Think about a group or team you belong to. It could be your family, your department at work, or an organization of which you are a member. Consider each person's role and relationship—with you and with each other—and determine where in the "puzzle" they are, and where they belong in the big picture.

Chapter 9 - July 7, 2005

Nothing to Fear

My birthday was last week, and one of the gifts I received was a colorful, handmade wall-hanging from a friend of mine who is one of the most creative people on the planet. It contained a quote by Gertrude Stein that read, "Everything in this world is so dangerous that it's silly to be afraid of anything."

You can read a lot into that statement, can't you? For starters, you could argue with it. After all, there *are* a lot of dangerous things in the world, and it seems to me that we *should* be afraid of them. If being afraid helps us to steer clear of places we shouldn't go, and things we shouldn't do, then fear serves a good purpose because it can help to protect us.

On the other hand, it can also paralyze us. It's easy to get paranoid when we think about all the random things that can happen in our day-to-day lives. All it takes is one quick encounter with a drunk driver—or a stray bullet or a wrong turn on a hiking trail—to turn something wonderful into something tragic. But if we stay away from everything that poses a possible threat to us, we'll never go anywhere or do anything at all.

I'm sure we've all taken part in the kind of conversation that starts with a tragic incident we've heard or read about, and expands to include other related occurrences. Pretty soon we start feeling as though we should never venture any farther from our house than the end of the block. Then we're brought back to reality when someone says, "But you know what? You can get killed just stepping off the curb. Or slipping in the shower. Or even getting out of bed."

The point is not that we should never even get out of bed. After all, it's possible you could get tangled up and strangled by the sheets—if you don't starve first. Rather, it's that you should never get so caught up in thinking about life's dangers that it keeps you from enjoying life's many delights.

There's a difference between avoiding something because we're afraid of it and avoiding it for any other reason. What we need to do is figure out which is which, and what we intend to do about it. For example, am I avoiding racecar driving and skydiving because they're dangerous, or because I truly have no interest in doing them? It's okay to have absolutely no desire to jump out of an airplane or negotiate hairpin turns at extremely high speeds. It's not okay, however, to miss out on a thrilling, exhilarating, exciting experience just because I'm afraid to try it.

And that goes for everything, not just things like, say, being afraid of breaking every bone in my body. Other fears involve different, less dramatic dangers, such as the fear of getting lost or rejected, or of falling, failing, or looking like an idiot.

I think my friend gave me a greater birthday gift than either one of us realized. She also gave me a challenge. Should I now examine my life, and figure out what I might have been missing because I've been afraid of it? Must I now realize that it's silly to let fear keep me safely tucked at home when there's a great big world out there to be explored and enjoyed? And do I now have to accept that the word "dangerous" means I may have to be careful and take precautions, but it's not an excuse to avoid doing anything?

Yep. I'm afraid so.

 Never get so caught up in thinking about life's dangers that it keeps you from enjoying life's many delights.

Find Another Nugget: What is something you've been wanting to try, but haven't yet? What fear or excuse has been stopping you? Try to identify it, name it, and figure out what you need to learn or do in order to overcome it. Then—go for it! Finally, enjoy the activity, as well as the satisfaction of just doing it.

Chapter 10 - July 28, 2005

Not On the Grocery List

I was in the grocery store the other day, heading for the checkout lane with a week's worth of groceries. As I approached the only empty lane in the store, another person was coming from the other direction, with a cart as loaded up as mine. We paused a moment, giving each other a chance to go first. He motioned for me to go ahead, which I did as he moved over to a different lane.

As I was leaving the store, I passed a woman who was just finishing bagging her groceries. Helping her was her son—the person who had been pushing the other grocery cart. He looked to be about 10 years old. I went up to the woman and told her what a courteous and polite son she had. In a situation where many people shift into demolition derby mode, he waited and gave me a chance to go ahead of him.

The woman looked surprised. Not, I assume, because her son did something nice, but because someone took the time to mention it.

"Thank you. I appreciate your saying that." I saw them again a few minutes later in the parking lot, because we were parked right next to each other. This time, the woman approached me.

"I really want to thank you for what you said in there," she told me, adding that her son was diabetic and his blood sugar was a little high that day, which sometimes makes him cranky. "He's still always polite, though."

As I started to get in my car, the son nodded and smiled at me. "Thank you," he said.

As I drove off into the sunset—well, actually in the other direction—I felt pretty darn good, although with a little twinge of guilt over getting in line ahead of a diabetic who was having a bad day. If I had known that, I'd certainly have let him go ahead of me in line. At least, I like to think I would.

While reflecting on all of this, I realized that what happened in the grocery store was a minor and insignificant event in the whole scheme of things. But it got me thinking about different times when I've picked up speed in order to beat someone else to the checkout line—or anywhere else—and how smug I felt when I did. I also thought about the times I've stewed, even for just a few minutes, after someone else beat me to the open lane, especially if they sped up and cut me off in order to get there first.

I thought about how good it felt, instead, to step back a moment and give someone else the opportunity to go first, and to have him step back and extend that same courtesy to me. I enjoyed how good it felt to let someone know that I noticed and appreciated his kindness, and then to feel his appreciation in return.

Courtesy, kindness, patience, gratitude, and appreciation aren't things I've ever put on my grocery list, or searched the shelves for as I filled up my shopping cart, but it seems they were an unannounced special at the grocery store last week.

And I realized they're worth waiting in line for.

 It feels good to let others know we notice and appreciate their kindness, and then to feel their appreciation in return.

Find Another Nugget: Try to notice someone—even better if it's a child—who's doing a kindness or courtesy for you or someone else. It can be as simple as holding a door open, or going out of their way to be helpful. Let them know that you noticed, by thanking them, complimenting them, or simply letting them know that you saw and admired what they did.

Chapter 11 - May 25, 2006

Failure Is Not an Option

What would you dare to try, if you knew you couldn't fail?

That's the question I had to answer during a recent Speech Contest at a Toastmasters District Conference, and I'm happy to report that I came up with a powerful, entertaining, and inspiring response to the question.

Unfortunately, however, it wasn't until several days after the contest, while I was at a gas station filling my tank, that I came up with this brilliant response. During the contest itself, my answer was only so-so.

But I've been thinking about the question ever since. It's an interesting one that offers up all sorts of possibilities, and it can teach us a little more about ourselves in the process.

What would *you* try doing, if you knew you couldn't fail?

Would it be something daring and dangerous, like jumping over the Grand Canyon on a motorcycle? Or something that's more of a financial risk than a physical one, like opening your own quilt shop or investing in a new computer company? Maybe you'd become a Broadway star, or a bestselling novelist, or you'd climb Mt. Everest.

Then again, you might decide to do something that benefits other people rather than yourself. Something noble, life-changing, and global in scope, like feeding the poor and sick and starving people around the world so that no child or adult ever goes to bed hungry again. That's what I came up with while I was pumping gas the other day. However, that answer immediately generated another question: How would I go about accomplishing this?

At this point, I realized what "can't fail" really means—because I also realized that even if I knew I couldn't fail at something, that doesn't mean it would happen automatically. I'd still have a lot of work to do, and I'd have to deal with more problems and overcome more obstacles than I could even begin to imagine.

Knowing that I couldn't fail, however, would be a pretty powerful motivator. Rather than slacking off or giving up when I hit a brick wall or a bump in the road, I'd work even harder and more diligently, knowing I had that ironclad guarantee.

Suddenly the words "confidence" and "determination" come to mind.

I don't need a speech contest or a hypothetical question in order to realize that if people are determined to do something, and they refuse to give up or to listen to anyone who says it can't be done, they're almost certain to succeed. If they believe that failure is not an option, then it isn't. One of my favorite quotes says, "You never fail until you stop trying."

I'm going to try to adopt that philosophy whenever I set out to accomplish something. Whether it's feeding the starving people of the world, starting my own business, climbing Mt. Everest, or winning a trophy at a future Toastmasters competition, all I need to know is that I can't fail.

All I need to do after that is work like crazy until I succeed.

If you believe that failure is not an option, then it isn't.

Find Another Nugget: What would you do if you knew you couldn't fail? Mentally walk through—or write down—all the steps it would take for you to actually accomplish it. As you're doing this, assume that you'd have all the money, time, help, and resources you need. Then take the first few steps and see what happens.

Chapter 12 - November 30, 2006

Be Happy

❝ Isn't it nice to be happy for someone you don't even know?"

A friend recently said this while we were having lunch with several other women after our monthly book club meeting. One of the women in our group had a small photo album of pictures from her son's wedding, which had taken place the month before. We were passing the album around as we ate, and each new person commented about what a beautiful couple the bride and groom made, how fabulous our friend—the mother of the groom—looked, and how much or how little of a family resemblance we could see in different people in the photos.

By the time the album had made its way around the table, we were all in a pretty festive mood. That's when my friend made her comment about being happy.

Yes, it's nice to be happy for someone you don't even know. It doesn't matter if it's a friend's son who just got married, or your sister-in-law's brother-in-law's cousin's daughter who just got a wonderful new job, or someone you simply read about who was reunited with a long-lost sibling. Knowing about someone else's good fortune, and being happy about it, can feel pretty good for us, too. And I'm willing to bet it has actual, physical benefits, like reducing stress, lowering blood pressure, and healthy things like that.

It's ironic that this happened on the same day that I woke up to a news report on my clock radio saying that the majority of middle-aged women do not consider themselves happy. I was too groggy first thing in the morning to catch the actual percentage they gave, but I was awake enough to hear the announcer continue on with the details, which started with the comment, "Women aged 35 to 55—."

That's the part that *really* woke me up, because according to their timetable, not only am I middle-aged—which didn't exactly come as a surprise—but I've got only a few years left before I graduate into the next category.

As you might guess, this did *not* make me happy.

For the record, the news report had to do with how overwhelmed and overloaded women in this age group are, with everyone and everything they have to take care of. At least I think that's what it was about. I was only half-listening, because I was still processing the information that I am living in the "middle ages," and that for me, they are almost over.

I guess I should look on the bright side. If it's middle-aged women who, as a group, are not happy, I have to assume that older women are. So I can start looking forward to that.

Actually, though, I have some questions and doubts about the report I heard on the radio. It sounds to me like it was more about exhaustion than a lack of happiness. The two can be related, certainly, but they're not the same thing.

They're not mutually exclusive, either. I'm sure we all can relate to feelings of happiness that come at the end of a project, a special occasion, or an event, even if we're exhausted from our efforts. The problem is that exhaustion can distract us from the joy, the satisfaction, and the happiness that are also part of the package, if only we'd pay closer attention. Maybe that's what we should be doing, no matter what age we are.

It *is* nice to be happy for people we don't even know. But it's even nicer to be happy for people we do know—and that includes ourselves.

Knowing about someone else's good fortune, and being happy about it, can feel pretty good for us, too.

Find Another Nugget: Actively seek out news about someone—someone you don't know personally—who has just experienced good fortune or who has cause for celebration. (You can browse through the newspaper or a magazine, or enter "Good news stories" into a search engine to find one online.) Think about how they got to this point, imagine how they are probably feeling, and make a conscious choice to be happy for them. Now, do the same for someone you *do* know personally.

Chapter 13 - May 31, 2007

A Truck, a Motorcycle, and Me

I was at a stoplight one day last week, at an intersection just off the freeway. In front of me was a guy on a motorcycle, and in front of him was somebody driving a pickup truck. It was a beautiful day, and the back window panel on the pickup was open. I wasn't paying much attention to either the truck or the motorcycle. I was just waiting for the light to change. Suddenly the guy on the motorcycle stood up and called out to the person in the pickup.

"Do you know you cut me off back there?"

The person in the truck—I couldn't see whether it was a man or a woman—said something in reply, but I didn't hear the actual words. Then the motorcycle guy said, "Just be careful, okay?"

The light turned green. The pickup truck drove through the intersection and turned right at the next corner. A few streets later, the motorcycle driver did the same. I continued driving until I got back to my house, all the while thinking, "What just happened here?"

I admit that when the guy on the motorcycle first called out to the person in the pickup truck, my mind raced ahead, wondering if there would be a verbal or physical altercation, if guns would be drawn and shots fired, or if the person in the pickup truck would do something like throw it into reverse and attempt to flatten the guy on the motorcycle.

I don't think any of this indicates that I have an overactive imagination or that I've been watching too much TV or too many action movies lately. The sad fact is that my concern came from stories of things that occur in the real world, similar incidents that have really happened and that I read about all too often.

That's why I was so surprised and impressed, not to mention relieved, by the motorcyclist's reaction and response to the whole thing. He wasn't looking for a fight, he didn't get angry to the point of violence—or even to the point of using a swear word—and he didn't act as though the person in the truck was a jerk. He called the driver's attention to an incident that could have caused an accident, and he asked the driver to be more careful in the future.

Then everyone drove off into the sunset.

I wish I could have heard what it was that the driver of the pickup truck said to the guy on the motorcycle. Was it that person's response—an apology, maybe, or at least the acknowledgment that he or she made a mistake or didn't see the motorcyclist—that diffused a potentially volatile situation? Or was the motorcycle driver just an easy-going guy in the first place, somebody who welcomed the opportunity to point out someone's dangerously poor judgment or inattention on the road, but didn't feel the need to make a big deal out of it or to allow his emotions to get out of control and turn it into a road rage incident?

I'll never know, and it really doesn't matter. Still, it felt good to get such a close-up view of an incident that could have gotten ugly but didn't, one that could have been a violent confrontation but wasn't, and one that gives me a chance to mention something we all should remember, but sometimes don't.

Be courteous and attentive to other drivers out on the road, and remember that such courtesy works both ways—whether you're in a pickup truck, on a motorcycle, or sitting behind them at a stoplight.

Be courteous and attentive to other drivers out on the road, and remember that such courtesy works both ways.

Find Another Nugget: The next time you're out in traffic and someone cuts you off, doesn't let you merge, or does something else that makes your blood boil, imagine a conversation you might have—a *civil* conversation—if you could talk to each other at the next stoplight. Visualize yourself calmly pointing out what they did wrong, and imagine them apologizing for being careless, distracted, or whatever else may have caused their poor judgment and bad behavior.

Chapter 14 - November 29, 2007

Fortune Cookie

I had lunch at a Korean restaurant with my dad and sister. The food was good, but the fortune in my fortune cookie was even better.

Okay, maybe it wasn't really better than the meal, but it was a whole lot better than my sister's fortune, which said something about enjoying sports. Mine, instead, said something that made me think and reflect, which is something I always enjoy. It read, "You see beauty in everyday things. Treasure this gift."

There certainly is beauty in the everyday things around us—in a sunrise or sunset, flowers in the garden, trees in autumn. Or a sparkling snowfall set against the backdrop of a dark night sky, which is beautiful even if we don't really want to see it or think about what it's going to look like by the time we have to go out in it the next morning.

The part of the fortune that really got me thinking was the part that said, "Treasure this gift." I never thought of it as a gift to be able to see beauty in everyday things. Even if beauty is in the eye of the beholder, I still don't think it takes a special talent or skill to be able to see it.

Maybe it does, though. Maybe it takes the kind of vision that young children have and that we often lose by the time we're adults—the kind that sees wonder and excitement and adventure everywhere, and that can make extraordinary discoveries even in the most ordinary of places. It's this same kind of vision that sees beauty in clouds on a rainy day, or in the empty, barren branches of a tree in the dead of winter.

A number of years ago, I worked with an illustrator who once told me that—contrary to popular belief—his talent was not in his hands, but in his eyes. He said that his gift was in how he saw things. His hand was just the tool that helped him recreate what he saw.

I think that was like my fortune cookie's message.

The way we see things *is* a gift. What we do with that is entirely up to us. My illustrator friend used his gift to create artwork and advertising. Another friend of mine, who sees colors and patterns and textures in ways that I would never be able to, uses her gift to create breathtakingly beautiful quilts. Photographers have the ability to see and compose a photograph, and they use their tools—cameras—to capture it. Several people I know have a special gift of being able to see, or sense, when someone else has a problem, and they always know just what to say or do to help.

Many people have such gifts, but don't think of them that way. I wish they would. Our views, our gifts, the things we take for granted because they're such a natural part of us, are things that can be of benefit not only to ourselves but to the people around us if we're willing to share our gifts with others, once we realize they are worth sharing.

I do see beauty in everyday things. I don't think that makes me unique or special, but I do think it's a gift I will appreciate—in fact, treasure—from now on. I don't quite see how I can use it to help anyone else, but I'll keep my eyes open for any opportunity.

Maybe some smart cookie will help me see the way.

 It's a gift to see beauty in everyday things. Treasure this!

Find Another Nugget: Walk around your home or neighborhood, and take a closer look at some of the everyday things you usually don't even notice. Study them. Find, acknowledge, and appreciate the beauty in them. Remind yourself that each of them is a gift, as is the opportunity to see and recognize this.

Chapter 15 - February 7, 2008

Be Persistent

I saw a guy fall flat on his face last week. Then I watched him pick himself up, climb right back up on the horse, so to speak, and do what he set out to do in the first place—beautifully, perfectly, and to thunderous applause.

While I was visiting my daughter in Florida, we attended a Cirque du Soleil show in Disney World. I've always wanted to see a Cirque du Soleil performance, but never had until now. Because of everything I've read, as well as from talking to people who have attended a show and from seeing snippets of performances on TV promotions, I couldn't wait to watch and enjoy the acrobatics, the costumes, the choreography, and the music of this famous troupe of performers.

I wasn't disappointed. In fact, the show exceeded my expectations many times over, and my adrenaline was pumping the whole time I was watching it. Each act seemed more stunning, daring, and entertaining than the last, and through it all was the sense of danger and risk that the performers were in during every moment they were on stage, or flying high above it. Even with the safety nets, harnesses, and spotters that were visible in the background, there was no doubt about the difficulty and danger in everything that was happening.

It was during the trapeze act that one of the performers slipped. He didn't literally fall flat on his face. What he did, literally, was fall flat on his back. He landed on the net, from which he bounced back up, acknowledged the audience—which had let out a collective gasp—and then moved off to the side of the stage and climbed back up to the performance area as the others continued their act.

A few minutes later, the same acrobat was back up and in place, ready to go for a second try. This time, he nailed it. The crowd roared and applauded, much louder and more enthusiastically than would have been the case had he completed the maneuver in the first place—partly in appreciation of a great feat, and partly in admiration for his coming back from a failed attempt and succeeding the second time around.

Few of us will ever fly through the air on a trapeze in front of hundreds or thousands of people. But most of us have had the experience, some of us more often than others, of falling flat on our faces or our backs when we've tried something new, pushed ourselves to the next level, or attempted to accomplish something we've never done before. Although we all know in our hearts that success comes from getting back up, trying again, and not quitting until we accomplish what we set out to do, I think we often forget that people actually recognize and respect that effort.

Too often we worry about what other people will say, or what they'll think of us when they see us fall or fail or not live up to the standards or goals we've set for ourselves. Unfortunately, that mindset can keep us from taking a chance, from going out on a limb, if not a trapeze, and from putting ourselves in a position where we might fail, especially if others might see it.

We need to get over that. We need to remember that persistence and determination are traits worth developing, and are traits people admire. They're also the ones that are most likely to bring us success, accomplishment, and personal satisfaction.

And, occasionally, thunderous applause.

Persistence and determination are traits that people admire, and that are most likely to bring us success, accomplishment, and personal satisfaction.

Find Another Nugget: Take a chance on something you've been afraid to start or to try. If you fall or fail, which is pretty common when we start something new, get back up and try again until you succeed, congratulating yourself for your persistence and determination.

Chapter 16 - December 11, 2008

A Wise Choice

" One of them had knowledge," my friend said, "and the other had wisdom."

She was talking about a doctor and nurse she had seen recently in advance of a medical procedure she needed to have done. She had not been to this particular medical office before. The doctor was good, which was her main concern, but he struck her as abrupt. It was the nurse who reassured her, answered her questions, and made her feel comfortable and confident about the procedure.

Her experience got us talking about healthcare in general, and how doctors have quotas to fill and paperwork to handle and an extremely limited amount of time to spend with each patient. We also talked about the difference between treating a patient and treating a person, and between education and experience.

If I had to name the difference between knowledge and wisdom, or between education and experience, I would say that knowledge and education come from books, while wisdom and experience come from people.

This is true not only in the medical profession, but in all walks of life. Some experts get their credentials through educational degrees, and some through real-world experience. Ideally and eventually, people will have both—at least the people with whom we trust our health, our cars and computers, and anything else we have that's in need of attention, treatment, or repair.

I think the operative word here is "trust." We want to know, or at least we need to believe, that the people taking care of us and of our belongings truly are caring for us and not looking at us simply as a number, a paycheck, or a part of their own daily routines and requirements. We need to know that we are being listened to, that we matter, and that our questions are being answered and our concerns are being addressed.

A study I read not long ago found that doctors who spent just a few more minutes with their patients had fewer lawsuits brought against them than other doctors did. In fact, there was a difference of three minutes between doctors who had never been sued at all and those who had been sued two or more times.

Theodore Roosevelt is credited with the quote, "People don't care how much you know until they know how much you care." I think we all would be wise to remember that. The knowledge we have can serve us well in our professional and personal lives, but it's the wisdom we acquire when we spend time with people that can make the biggest difference in their lives and in ours.

> We can get knowledge and education from books, but we get wisdom and experience from people.

Find Another Nugget: Look at one specific area of your life—your job, a hobby or leisure activity, or raising your children. Think about how much of it came from education such as classes or training, reading or research, and how much of it came from your personal experience and involvement. Recognize the combination of knowledge and wisdom that brought you to where you are today, and note which is more important or matters most to you now.

Chapter 17 - January 15, 2009

Mark the Calendar

My calendar is back—the little pocket-sized one that I used to keep on the kitchen desk or counter, and where I would mark down things like how many glasses of water I drank every day, how many servings of fruits and vegetables I ate, and on how many days of the week I exercised.

I started noting these things years ago, and kept it up for a long time. It all started when I decided to challenge myself to try one new recipe a week, and I wanted to keep track of how well I was doing. Until that point, I was always cutting recipes out of newspapers and magazines, but rarely getting around to actually trying them. Now I was going to make a game of it. So I took all the recipes I had stuffed into one big envelope, and sorted them into broad categories. Then it was easy to pick out a new main dish, side dish, appetizer, or dessert to try. Some of those recipes became family favorites, while others were tossed out after trying them just once. But they all got marked down on the calendar.

Realizing that I wasn't drinking as much water as I should, or eating as many fruits and vegetables as we're supposed to every day, I decided to add those to my "log book," both as a way to see how many and how much I was already eating and drinking, and as an incentive to do more. It wasn't a lot of trouble to keep track of them. I simply left the calendar out in the open, and made a little mark on the correct date every time I did something I was supposed to do.

Over the years, I added or changed the things I kept track of, like the daily sit-ups I started to do while I watched *Jeopardy!*—exercising both my mind and my body at the same time. And how many hours of sleep I got each night, when I realized I had been staying up way too late, way too often. I even decided once to make a point of doing a good deed every day, and marking that down on my calendar. I soon changed my mind, though—not about doing good deeds, but about keeping track of them. I didn't like the feeling it gave me that I was doing something nice for others simply to meet my quota, rather than just for the sake of being nice.

Two years ago, I decided to quit the calendar habit altogether. I figured I'd been doing it long enough that the good habits it promoted were pretty much a part of me, and I didn't need a calendar, or the chore of keeping track of everything, in order to make sure I did them.

But it turns out I do.

There wasn't a sudden or noticeable change. I didn't switch from water to Coke and Mountain Dew. I didn't toss out all the frozen vegetables in my freezer and replace them with frozen French fries. But gradually, over the course of time, I started slipping up on my intake of the good stuff, and indulging in more of the bad stuff. My weight didn't balloon, but it did start creeping up, and I found myself feeling a little more sluggish, a little more often. I realize that part of this can come simply with growing older, but I don't like it, and I don't have to accept it because I know I can do something about it.

I've also come to realize the sad truth that bad habits are easy to make and difficult to break, while the opposite is true for good habits. When we find some tricks and tools that help us make and maintain the good ones, we should hang on to them.

So my calendar is back, streamlined and updated for 2009. I'm not keeping track of new recipes anymore, or things like reading a book every week. I may add such things later on, but right now it's just the basics: water, fruits and veggies, exercise, and hours of sleep. I started at the beginning of the year, and I've noticed a difference already—first in my mind and my attitude, which is where the most effective changes have to start. As my body catches up, I'll also know it by how I look and feel, and by the number of marks on my calendar.

Bad habits are easy to make and difficult to break, while the opposite is true for good habits. So when we find some tricks and tools that help us make and maintain the good ones, we should hang on to them.

Find Another Nugget: What's a good habit you'd like to develop? What tips or tricks can you incorporate to help you establish and continue it? Start them now.

Chapter 18 - September 17, 2009

A Chill in the Air

"It's great sleeping weather."

These words kept popping into my head one night recently, as I was driving to town on a late-evening errand. It had been warm during the day, and I left my car window open when I returned home and pulled into the garage that afternoon. I kept it open now, although it was after 8:00 at night and the air was brisk and chilly. Still, it felt good. It was, indeed, great sleeping weather.

This is the time of year when my husband and I go through the annual ritual of noting how much shorter the days are getting, and how quickly it seems to be happening.

"Look how dark it is," one of us will say to the other. "And it's only ___ o'clock." We fill in the blank with times that get earlier and earlier every few days. On this night I would have said, "It's just after 8:00, and already it's pitch-black."

Over the course of time, this ritual is balanced by its opposite—the one we enjoy more as we look forward to the coming of summer—when we note in the springtime how much lighter it is at earlier and earlier times in the evening.

It may seem silly for us to keep mentioning this and pointing out the obvious, especially with regard to something that happens every year at the same time and is not subject to political, economic, or industrial influences. Maybe that's why we do it. There's a comfort in knowing this is something we recognize, something we can count on, something that's familiar, even when it means we're heading into the cold, dark months of winter.

Winter won't arrive for a while yet. It's a gradual process, even though it sometimes doesn't seem that way here in Minnesota. But in between now and then, we have our end-of-summer activities and the rituals of autumn to anticipate. These aren't as regular and unchangeable as the seasons and the laws of nature that govern daylight hours, though. They're more reflective of our personal lives, and of our circumstances and preferences—the start of the school year, football season, and changing the closets from summer clothes to winter clothes.

For me, this time of year always brings back memories—as well as the scents and sounds—of marching bands and bonfires, of apples and pumpkins that will soon turn into taffy apples and jack-o-lanterns. It's the time of year when I start thinking about trying out new soup recipes, and about whipping up a batch of hot buttered rum mix, which I store in the refrigerator all winter and use for warm, sweet drinks on cold Sunday nights.

Autumn is the comforting time of year. Maybe that becomes more important to me as I get older, although age may have nothing to do with it. Maybe it's just that it feels so safe and secure, and so warm and welcoming. It feels like a dear friend who will always be here for me, no matter what else is going on in my life, and no matter what changes may have occurred since last fall, or are on the road up ahead.

Perhaps it's this feeling, even more than the chill in the air and the ever-darkening nights, that makes for great sleeping weather.

 There's comfort in having something we recognize, something we can count on, something familiar.

Find Another Nugget: What's your favorite season? What is it about that time of year that gives you comfort and pleasure? Make a point of enjoying the feeling of familiarity it brings. Try to do the same as each new season begins.

Chapter 19 - March 11, 2010

Hero and Mentor

❝ The ability to be a hero, and an obligation to be a mentor."

I came across this phrase recently, and it really stayed with me. I've been thinking about what it means, what it would involve, and what it would be like if every one of us took it seriously. There's no doubt in my mind that it would have a positive, powerful, and noticeable effect, both in our individual lives and in the world around us.

Although we may not realize it, we all have the ability to be a hero. This doesn't mean we have to demonstrate super-human strength, or perform brave deeds that put our lives in danger and our names in the headlines. It means we have to act and behave in ways that other people can look up to, can believe in, and can learn from—ways that can make a difference in their lives by inspiring them, by encouraging them, by influencing them. People become heroes to others in different ways and for different reasons. Quite often, it's not so much because of some great feat they've done, but because of what they had to overcome in order to do it.

I've never considered myself to be the "hero" type of person. I'm more the "nurturing and support" type, but years ago, after I recovered from breast cancer, a number of people told me I was their hero. Either they or someone close to them had just found out they had cancer, or they feared a possible diagnosis of cancer because of medical tests or symptoms they were undergoing. The fact that I not only survived, but was living a happy and fulfilling life afterwards, was an inspiration to them. It gave them the hope, the encouragement, and the reassurance they needed.

I felt a bit guilty about being called a hero. I didn't think I had done anything to deserve it; I was simply handling as best I could the situation I faced. Yet knowing people thought of me that way gave me an increased sense of purpose. It made me feel that I had the responsibility to recover fully and live well not only for myself and my family, but for those who needed a role model or a reminder that they could do it, too.

Think of some of the people you consider to be heroes. Include your own personal heroes, not just the famous, larger-than-life ones. What about them makes them a hero to you, and why is that important? Very likely it has to do with something you can relate to, such as a challenge or struggle you're going through in your own life, or a way of living to which you aspire. Now look at it from the other direction and see that you, indeed, have the power and the ability to be a hero to someone else.

Serving as a mentor is even easier than being a hero, although it may take a bit more time, as well as a conscious decision and an active commitment. Still, it doesn't mean we have to enroll in a formal mentoring program or take on specific people to mentor. It also doesn't mean we give away for free the kind of training, teaching, or trade secrets that deserve compensation or need to be learned or acquired on one's own. It simply means sharing what we know, and what we've learned, with other people who could benefit from that knowledge. It means guiding them in ways that won't deplete or diminish us in any way, but will give them some help and resources that can make their own life's journey a little easier. Often, it's simply a matter of giving some advice or an opinion, suggesting a website or an organization, or sharing a story about an experience of our own, and what resulted from it.

Many people say they don't have the time to mentor others, or that the world is so competitive and cut-throat that they would never want to, because someone they helped up the ladder could later knock them off of it. I think mentoring relationships foster more of a collaborative relationship than a competitive one. Whenever I've mentored anyone, formally or informally, I've usually ended up learning and benefiting more from the experience than the person I was mentoring.

Realizing that my actions and experiences can make me a hero to other people, and knowing that whenever I help someone else I end up helping myself even more, I can see how "the ability to be a hero and the obligation to be a mentor" can make me a better and stronger person, with a goal of being of service to others, but with an outcome that also improves my own life. It's something I'm going to start incorporating into my life whenever I can. I hope you will, too.

Whenever you help someone else, you end up helping yourself even more.

Find Another Nugget: Think of some of the people you consider to be heroes. Then determine why you look up to them—what about them makes them seem heroic? What can you do to be that kind of hero to someone else?

Chapter 20 - September 23, 2010

A Funny Smell

Insights, observations, and life lessons sometimes come from the strangest places. Like my refrigerator.

Not long ago, I noticed a funny smell coming from the fridge. Although it doesn't happen very often anymore—not since the days when both of my kids were living at home and the refrigerator regularly held way more food than it does now—every once in a while some little bit of fruit or leftovers will get pushed to the back and hidden behind a larger container. There it will sit, quiet and forgotten, until it turns into a "science experiment" and makes itself known.

That's what I figured must have happened, so the first thing I did was to move everything on each of the shelves in order to find the offending food. Nothing I could see was causing the problem. Next I checked the drawers and bins, and the jars and bottles in the door of the fridge. Still nothing. So I decided to do a full overhaul. I was a little overdue, anyway, for cleaning out the entire refrigerator.

One shelf at a time, I took all the food out of the fridge. I removed the shelves, separated the pieces that came apart, washed and disinfected everything, then reassembled the pieces. I scrubbed out the inside of the refrigerator, wiped down all the food containers, and rearranged everything as I put it back in the fridge.

I never did figure out exactly what was causing the bad smell, but it was gone by the time I finished cleaning. When I was done, I stood for a moment—as I always do when I've completed a clean-up or decluttering project, no matter where in the house it is—and took a look at my handiwork. I enjoyed and admired how spotless and organized everything looked, and in this case, I also enjoyed noticing how fresh and clean it smelled.

However, I noticed something else, too. Even though I had tossed out some items that were just about past their prime, and even with no leftovers waiting to be consumed or specific ingredients gathered together to prepare for that evening's dinner, the refrigerator was still pretty full. That's when I was struck with a profound realization:

Life is like a refrigerator.

Sometimes it gets stuffed with so many different things that a few of them get lost, pushed aside, and forgotten. That may seem harmless enough, but if we don't take care of them and finish them off—or dispose of them properly when their usefulness has passed—they can cause problems that come back to haunt us. The remnants left behind can seep into newer and fresher things, and can spoil them. At the very least, they take up space and energy that can be better used in other ways and for other purposes. And at worst, they can cause damage or destruction, or just take the fun out of everything else.

We may also find that we simply have too much of a good thing. A refrigerator that's filled with different types of sauces and spices, exotic condiments, fancy mustards, jams, and cheeses can leave your mouth watering for something of substance that you still can't find. You can have a full refrigerator, but nothing to eat, just as you can have a jam-packed closet, but nothing to wear, or a day filled with busy activities, but nothing that really gets accomplished.

When we start noticing this, it's time to let go of some things, even if they haven't reached their expiration date, and even if they still fit and are still in style. It's time to let go even if they're enjoyable and useful activities, but they don't help us accomplish what we really want to get done.

I'm not emptying out my refrigerator, my closet, or my calendar in one fell swoop. However, I *am* trying to weed out and get rid of what I no longer need, what doesn't work for me anymore, or what other people can get more use or enjoyment out of than I can at this point in my life. I know it can be done quickly or gradually, and I'll do it at the pace that works best for me. As I go along, I'll remember that the more I pare down in any area of my life, the more I'll be able to use and enjoy whatever is left.

I think this is food for thought that will take some time to digest, so the first thing I'll do is take another look inside my clean, fresh, organized refrigerator. It will serve as a reminder of what I intend to do. It will give me a renewed sense of inspiration and motivation.

And it will allow me to figure out what I'm going to fix for dinner.

The more we pare down in any area of our lives, the more we'll be able to use and enjoy whatever is left.

Find Another Nugget: Identify an area of your life, home, or work that is overstuffed or overcrowded. What do you need to do to pare it down or clear it out? Whether it's a drawer or cabinet that won't quite close, a to-do list that's a mile long, or a project with too many moving parts, set aside an afternoon, evening, or weekend to tackle the job.

Chapter 21 - January 13, 2011

A Christmas Candle

Sometimes it's a lightbulb that goes off with a flash of brilliance, giving us an innovative and exciting new idea. For me, it was a candle.

Specifically, it was a scented candle that I received as a Christmas gift. It has become part of a new daily practice for me, one that has already put more peace and pleasure into my morning, and more productivity and efficiency into the rest of my day.

I used to start my workday by sitting down at my computer and getting right down to business, starting with what was most important or what was screaming the loudest. Now, instead, I gather up all the notes, papers, lists, and other materials that relate to whatever I'm working on or preparing to start. I spread everything out on my kitchen table, along with a handful of file folders and envelopes, a pen and notepad, and my calendar. Then I make myself a cup of green tea, light my new candle, and sit down to look at everything I've got coming up. I organize and prioritize my projects and tasks. I make whatever new notes or reminders I need. Next I figure out what is the best time of day to do each of the things I need to do. Only then—and after blowing out the candle—do I return to my desk and get to work. I'm more focused, relaxed, and confident, I'm able to get more done in less time, and I find the entire day more enjoyable and fulfilling.

Although I always knew the value of organizing and prioritizing, I didn't always take the time to do it. Often, I didn't think I *had* the time, because there were urgent matters I needed to tend to right away, or deadlines that were fast approaching. But now, I've turned this chore into a treasured morning ritual, and I actually feel a pang of regret when the organizing is finished and it's time to blow out the candle.

It is our daily practices that determine whether or not we'll reach our goals, complete our plans, and achieve our dreams. When our daily practices are enjoyable in and of themselves, we are much more likely to continue doing them, which is the fastest path to success—no matter what we're working on or we hope to accomplish.

Very soon, I'll be packing up my Christmas candle and putting it away with the rest of our Christmas decorations. Before I do, however, I'll select another candle to use each morning as I continue my new tradition. It may not be a scented candle, as this one was, but I know it will still keep me on task as I start each new day. It will also allow me to enjoy—more quickly and more often—the sweet smell of success.

It is our daily practices that determine
whether or not we'll reach our goals,
complete our plans, and achieve our
dreams. When our daily practices
are enjoyable in and of themselves,
we are much more likely to continue
doing them.

Find Another Nugget: What is something you've been meaning to do for a long time, but haven't yet managed to get done—or even started? Carve out a daily block of time, preferably first thing in the morning or last thing at night, and design a ritual around it. This should be something that you can enjoy doing, that entices you not to skip it when time is short, and that can become an automatic habit. Establishing the routine is your first goal; accomplishing whatever you set out to do is your second.

Chapter 22 - February 10, 2011

Coming or Going

I was in my forties when my husband, kids, and I moved from the Chicago area—where we were born and raised—to Roanoke, Virginia. It was the first of several moves we made to different parts of the country. After a few months of living in Virginia, one of my neighbors asked, "So, Betty, are you starting to like it here in Roanoke, or do you still miss Chicago?"

My one-word answer: "Yes."

I didn't see the two as mutually exclusive. I was very much enjoying Roanoke, and exploring this new part of the country, but I missed my family and friends and all that was familiar "back home."

What made me think of this recently is that in the last few weeks I've started working with two new coaching clients, and I have two other clients who just finished the program. In a way, my feelings are the same as when we first moved to Roanoke. I'm always eager to start the program again, and I love helping new clients explore and enjoy the vast new world of opportunities and possibilities that is opening up to them. But I hate saying goodbye to them when the program comes to a close, and I'm no longer in contact with them on a weekly or bi-weekly basis.

As with moving from Chicago, however, I've learned that moving to a different place does not mean leaving behind everything or everyone from the past. Even though my relationship with clients changes once we've finished working together, it continues on in a different way. In many cases, we've stayed in touch through email, occasional phone calls, and an on-line coaching community. I also remain a permanent member of the team of people they know they can count on for ideas, advice, input, and assistance. As they continue to pursue their goals and dreams, I often feel like a proud mother watching them. And I'm thrilled to be a part of the process, whether it's from up close and personal during the coaching program or from more of a distance after it's done.

Finishing up in one area—whether it's moving, completing a program, or fulfilling one dream and starting in on another—does not mean "The End." It usually means the beginning, and everything you take with you as you begin anew will include the lessons you've learned, the experience you've gained, and the relationships you've formed.

I have to remind myself of this from time to time, especially since it relates to so many areas of life. Our families change as kids grow up and go off to start new lives and families of their own. We move to new places in terms of our homes, our jobs, the organizations to which we belong, and the activities in which we take part. When it's time to say goodbye, it helps to remember that there's a great big "Hello" when we turn around and look in the other direction. When we can do that, we're able to treasure the memories of everywhere we've been, enjoy where we are right now, and look forward eagerly and with sweet anticipation to wherever we'll be going next.

 Finishing something does not mean "The End." It usually means the beginning.

Find Another Nugget: With the start of any new plan or project, imagine its successful conclusion, and think about what that will look and feel like to you. When any plan or project is coming to a close, see it as a new beginning, and envision what it can launch you into next.

Chapter 23 - November 1, 2012

How You Spin It

❝ You're passionate about what you're doing, and you really care about the people you're working with.❞

I'd love to tell you this was said about me, but it wasn't. It was said to my friend Ruth, and she shared it with me when we got together to catch up on what's been going on in our lives.

Ruth is an indoor cycle instructor. She leads classes at the fitness centers where she works, and she is so good at what she does, and so passionate about it, that I feel like I've gotten a good workout just by listening to her talk.

It all started several years ago, when she took a cycle class and got hooked on the experience. She became even more enthusiastic as she started losing weight and gaining strength, stamina, and everything else that comes when we start exercising vigorously and consistently. But this wasn't really what set her in motion—no pun intended—to be a cycle instructor. It was simply the joy she got from cycling.

When she first started training to become a certified instructor, Ruth had a lot of doubts about how successful she could be at it. For one thing, she had to invest a fair amount of time and energy in the training itself. For another, most instructors already had a loyal following of class participants, and it could take a while to build up her own clientele. There is more to cycle classes than simply cycling. The personality of the instructors, the type of playlist they put together for their classes, and the level and degree to which they push the participants all make cycle classes as individual and unique as the instructors themselves.

Ruth needn't have worried. A year after she acquired her certification and began teaching, the number of classes she was leading increased from two to twelve, and she now teaches water aerobics as well as cycling. She has continued to receive training and certification in other disciplines, including as a group fitness instructor, which qualifies her to teach classes in any number of different types of exercise.

"The more I learn," she told me, "the more there is that I realize I need to learn. And the more I learn, the better able I am to help the people in my classes."

As we talked, I became more and more fascinated and impressed with all the classes she has taken, and the continuing education she is receiving—anatomy and physiology, health and nutrition, teaching styles and methods, and on and on. I have a feeling that by the time she's done, she'll be qualified not only to teach exercise, but to perform heart surgery.

There are two different ways Ruth, or any of us, could look at this. One would be to get frustrated, overwhelmed, and discouraged by the amount of knowledge and training involved. The other is to be eager, excited, and motivated by it.

I think it's obvious which one applies to my friend. She truly wants to learn as much as she can because she is so passionate about every aspect of it. Also, a large part of the incentive for her is her genuine concern for the participants in her classes. She wants them to get as much benefit as they can, in an environment that is as safe and enjoyable as possible.

It was the master trainer in her group fitness instructor class, by the way, who made the observation that she knew Ruth was going to be successful because she was passionate about what she was doing and she really cared about the people she was working with.

I can think of no better way for any of us to determine or improve our chances for success—in our careers, our relationships, or any area of our lives—than to ask ourselves those two questions: Are we passionate about what we're doing? Do we genuinely care about the people we are working with?

If we can answer "Yes" to both questions, then we, like Ruth, have the ability and the capacity to succeed beyond our wildest dreams.

If not, we may simply be spinning our wheels.

Ask yourself these two questions: Am I passionate about what I'm doing? Do I genuinely care about the people I am working with? Answering "Yes" to both can determine or improve your chances for success.

Find Another Nugget: Ask yourself these two questions about every aspect of your life. If the answer to both of them is a resounding "Yes!" that's great! If one or both answers is "No," think about what you could change—and it could simply be your attitude— that would transform "No" into "Yes." If you can't come up with a single thing, spend some time in reflection imagining what would have to take place in order for you to be passionate about what you were doing, and to care about the people with whom you were working.

Chapter 24 - November 15, 2012

Treasures All Around Us

I'm always amazed when I see, for the first time, something that was right in front of me all along. Sometimes I even have to laugh at the irony. Such was the case a while ago with a coffee mug I had owned and been using for several years. On the mug is a scene from nature—snow-capped mountains alongside a forest of deep green pine trees, and the rushing waters of a flowing river lined by rugged boulders. Eagles are soaring, fish are jumping, and clouds are floating lazily by. The caption on the mug says, "Discover the wonder in every day!"

I enjoy the image, and I'm inspired by the message. I have no idea how many cups of coffee and tea I drank from that mug, however, before I noticed there were other images hidden among the obvious ones. Camouflaged within the stunning outdoor setting were outlines of a bear, a wolf, several more fish and eagles, and a few other animals that make their home in mountains, forests, and streams. Today when I look at that coffee mug, these "hidden" images jump out at me, and I can't believe I didn't see them earlier.

Last week I had a similar experience with a shirt I've owned for several years, and that I wear every few weeks. It's a blue V-neck pullover with a black design printed on it. It's a nondescript design that reminds me of Japanese silhouette art. It almost looks as though someone dipped a paintbrush in black ink and then spattered the ink onto the shirt.

Words are incorporated into the design, blended so well into the background that they appear to be part of the scenery, like the animals hidden in the picture on my coffee mug. The "ink spatters" obscure some of the writing, so it's a bit difficult to decipher even if you're paying attention to it, which I had never really done before.

I don't know what made me stop and actually read the words as I was putting on the shirt last week, but I was astonished when I did. The message said, "A world of opportunity awaits those brave enough to take the path less followed."

I could have added, "Or who take the time to notice it."

It was a little embarrassing to realize that this profound message and excellent advice was right in front of me, literally, every time I had worn this shirt, but it had taken me so long to notice it. Later on, when I was telling a friend about my big revelation, she provided me with another one.

"Things will be revealed to us when the time is right," she said. "I think it's one of the ways God talks to us. We pray and ask for answers, and we always want them right now. Instead, they're given to us as we need them, and when we're ready to receive them."

I like this idea a whole lot better than thinking I miss things that are right in front of me because I'm so distracted or rushed that I don't even see them. Either way, however, the point is well taken. There is much wonder to be discovered, and many treasures to be found, in our everyday lives—as long as we're paying attention, are willing to explore, and are ready to receive them.

I'm going to remind myself of this whenever I can. It's a great message to carry with me as I travel through life—as I'm getting dressed each morning, as I'm going about my business during the day, and as I'm reflecting on my achievements every evening.

And, certainly, whenever I'm enjoying a quiet cup of coffee.

There are many treasures to be found in our everyday lives—as long as we're paying attention, are willing to explore, and are ready to receive them.

Find Another Nugget: Focus your attention on something you see or do every day, to the point where you take it for granted. It could be an object such as a picture hanging on your bedroom wall, or the lamp you turn on when you sit down to read or watch TV. Or it could be an activity such as having a cup of coffee or brushing your teeth. Take a few minutes to actively study it, analyzing how it looks, how it feels, and what it does to you or for you. Try to notice it as if it's something brand new to you. Is there something hidden in the object or activity that you can now enjoy and appreciate in a new way?

Chapter 25 - February 21, 2013

Dancer or Cheerleader?

"Were you ever a dancer?" my doctor asked during my annual physical a few weeks ago. I was surprised and flattered by the question.

"No," I said. "But thanks for asking."

"A cheerleader?" he continued, which made me laugh. I've never been particularly athletic or coordinated, and the closest I ever came to cheerleading was being in the marching band in high school.

I asked him why he thought I may have been a dancer or cheerleader, and he explained that as he was testing my reflexes and flexibility, he noted that mine were better than those of most people my age. I ignored the "my age" part, and simply took pride in the fact that I could be mistaken for someone who was a dancer or cheerleader years ago.

Feeling rather pleased with myself as I left the doctor's office, I started thinking about the contributing factors to my "condition." I decided that working out at Curves, which I do four or five days a week, probably had the most to do with it. Also, I'm interested in health and nutrition in general, and I try to follow a healthy diet most of the time.

But then something else occurred to me, and I wasn't sure at first whether it was a good thing or a bad thing.

The "thing" that occurred to me was my motivation. I'd love to claim that I simply value a healthy mind and body, and that I actively and aggressively follow a diet and exercise program that helps me to do and be my best at all times. While this is true to a certain degree, it's not my main motivation.

My main motivation—although I never really thought about it like this before—is fear and avoidance, which is not nearly as noble or glamorous.

A number of years ago, following chemotherapy for breast cancer, I developed severe heart damage that still affects me today. It doesn't slow me down anymore, and it doesn't keep me from doing anything I really want to do. However, its effects were permanent, and I'm always aware that if I get a little too careless about what or how much I'm eating and drinking, or if I slack off a little in my exercise routine, the effects could be much more severe than they would be for the average person with a normal, healthy heart.

That scares me. It's something I want to avoid at all costs, and it's what motivates me to keep exercising regularly, to pay attention to my diet and lifestyle, and to make an appointment every year for my annual physical, as well as for any other tests and procedures that are warranted.

What I find the most interesting is the realization that I probably wouldn't be as strict or vigilant about all this if I hadn't had that combination of cancer, chemo, and heart damage years ago. I probably wouldn't be as interested in health and nutrition as I am, or as committed to exercising and staying in shape. I'm certain I wouldn't have people asking me now if I had ever been a dancer or cheerleader.

Sometimes it's not the good things that happen to us, but rather the bad things, that help us the most in the long run. That doesn't make them any easier to deal with while we're going through them. But if we're aware of this, it can give us hope for the future—even if we never really learn or appreciate it until we get far enough into the future to recognize it.

I guess I'm there now, at least with respect to my heart, my health, my flexibility, and my reflexes. That's certainly something worth cheering about. In fact, it makes me feel like dancing.

Sometimes it's not the good things that happen to us, but rather the bad things, that help us the most.

Find Another Nugget: Think about a difficult or painful situation you had to deal with in the past, such as a medical crisis, a professional setback, or a personal disappointment. In hindsight, focus on the lessons it taught you, the strength it gave you, or the new paths it opened up for you.

Chapter 26 - April 4, 2013

Life in Harmony

Balance.

It's what many people today wish for, work toward, and try to achieve. Most of us would like to have more balance in our lives, but life today is busier than ever, with more demands on our time and energy. We spend much of our time being pulled in many directions, and few of us ever seem to achieve the balance we're seeking.

Maybe we're looking for the wrong thing.

Say the word "balance," and I picture an old circus act in which a performer would start a number of plates spinning around, balanced on top of tall sticks, and then run from one to another to keep them spinning so the plates wouldn't fall and break. Or I think of a tightrope walker—as long as we're referring to circus acts—inching his way along the high wire. Or, closer to home and more down to earth, I imagine someone standing on one foot, arms outstretched, constantly shifting his weight slightly in order to stay upright without having to put the other foot down.

This is not how I want to spend my life, especially now that I found something better to strive for. It's not balance, but harmony.

I realized this during a recent coaching session. My client is also a personal friend whom I've known long enough to be aware of the many different activities and projects she's been involved in over the last few years. During one of our sessions, we were exploring different things that motivate and excite her. Musical words and phrases kept coming up, especially "harmony."

What occurred to us both is that harmony is a form of balance, but it doesn't involve equal time for everything, or making sure we don't drop the ball on anything as we go about our day. Harmony doesn't necessitate giving up some of the things we do and enjoy in order to do a better job on the ones that are more important. And it's not about preventing things from crashing to the ground or falling through the cracks. It's about getting everything working together so we can create a rich, satisfying life.

I'm working really hard here to keep from saying "so we can make beautiful music," but that actually sums it up.

Think about a symphony orchestra—or a rock band, if that's more your style. Either way, there are a number of different voices and instruments. They all play a part, but not all at the same time, or in equal measure. Some almost always carry the melody. They're usually front and center, getting the most attention. Others stay in the background most of the time, but come to the forefront when needed. Some are silent for long periods of time, but when it's their turn to shine, they do.

It's worth noting that without direction, the same voices and instruments that sound so pleasing together might instead produce nothing but noise and annoyance. What they need is someone who knows the score and who coordinates their roles, someone who understands what they are and what they are capable of, and someone who can blend the strengths of each of them into something amazing.

That would be you.

The voices and instruments are the different parts of your life. Sure, you can keep trying to balance them, but getting them in harmony will be much more enriching and rewarding.

My friend and coaching client is now seeing or implementing harmony into pretty much everything she does. It even showed up while she was vacationing recently, and getting her hair done at a new salon.

(She and her hairdresser had a conversation about "Harmony Hair," but that's another story.)

I asked her if I could write about her experience, and she gave me both her permission and her blessing.

"Share it with as many people as you can," she told me. "The more people who are in harmony with each other, the better we'll all be."

Her words were generous, inspiring, and encouraging—and music to my ears.

The more people who are in harmony with each other, the better we'll all be.

Find Another Nugget: Imagine the different parts of your life as musical instruments in an orchestra. Which are playing the loudest right now, and carrying the main melody? Which are providing accents or undercurrents? Are any of them overpowering the others, or resting now until it's their turn to join in? What changes do you need to make in order to bring everything into harmony?

Chapter 27 - February 27, 2014

Letting Go

I spent last weekend at my dad's house, which is the house we moved into when I was nine years old, and that defines for me the word "home" in conversations about going home for the holidays.

The main reason for the visit was to help celebrate my nephew's 13th birthday on Saturday, and to attend the rock concert he was performing in on the same day. He's been taking guitar lessons for about four years, and every three or four months, the school arranges concerts so that students not only learn to play an instrument, they get real-life stage experience in front of audiences that include people other than just their parents and grandparents. I had a great time at the concert, and my nephew was in the set that featured Beatles Number One Hits, which made it even better.

Although Saturday was for celebrating, that wasn't the only reason for our visit, and the rest of the weekend was more sad and somber. This was the first visit back to my dad's house since his funeral a few weeks ago, and my sisters and I have started the process of going through fifty years' worth of memories and memorabilia, as well as clothing, furnishings, and paperwork.

Our weekend included visits and appointments with bankers, realtors, and Dad's tax accountant, as well as time spent going through each room in the house—sorting, organizing, and determining which items each of us might want to have, and what to do with everything else. We tried to separate the trash from the treasures, and to figure out what to keep, what to sell, what to give away or donate, and what to toss.

It was a difficult and emotional job, but we tried to lighten it up whenever we could. We watched some of the Olympics while we folded and packed up bags of clothing for Goodwill. We also joked, as we started in on each new room or closet, about whether this might be where we would find the lottery ticket worth a million bucks, or a dusty painting that would turn out to be a Rembrandt or Monet.

Mostly, though, we worked quietly, sorting through things as quickly and efficiently as we could, stopping every so often—very often, actually—when we came upon something that triggered a special memory or brought some fuzzy, distant aspect of our family's history clearly and brightly into focus. I spent a little extra time going through the cards and photos from the surprise party we threw for my dad on his 75th birthday, and whenever I found anything related to my mom, who died more than 40 years ago.

We got a lot done in the three days we spent going through the house, but there's more to be done. Some tasks we can do from a distance, such as making certain decisions and arrangements, but some will require additional time at Dad's house.

I still feel his presence when I'm there. It's a feeling that's both joyful and sad, and it's something I'm not quite ready to give up. I've always had a hard time letting go and saying goodbye, and this is one of the most difficult ones of my life.

I know this is what most people go through when they have to let go not only of a loved one, but of a place that's been home for many, many years. I also know that death is part of life, that our houses—as well as our bodies—are only temporary living quarters, and that our greatest treasures are our memories, not our possessions.

I'll be making a few more trips to Dad's house before we get everything finished and settled. I'm guessing that each trip will be a little easier in some ways and more difficult in others, and also that I'll always think of it as "Dad's house," no matter who else might be living there.

I'm sure that as I finally let go of the house and all its connections to my dad, I'll be able to hold on even more to the memories I have of him. Those thoughts will always take me home.

 Our memories, not our possessions, are our greatest treasures.

Find Another Nugget: Is there something or someone you're having difficulty letting go of or saying goodbye to? Look for ways to process or preserve the good memories related to that person or possession.

Chapter 28 - October 16, 2014

The Small, Quiet Ones

One morning last week, I set my alarm extra early so I could see the stellar event I'd been reading about: the "blood moon" and eclipse scheduled for the wee hours of the morning. The eclipse was interesting to watch, but the deep red color the moon was supposed to be didn't live up to its hype. That's okay, though. Just the act of getting up to see it made me think, as these events always do, about the days when my daughter still lived at home, and we'd go out in the back yard together to watch for meteor showers, lunar eclipses, and planets lining up in ways they did only once every 500 years or so. Those memories alone—not of the events themselves, but of the pleasure of searching the night sky for them with my daughter—were worth losing a little sleep that morning.

I found myself staring up at the sky on another day not long ago, about a week before the lunar eclipse. This time it was in broad daylight, and there was no advance warning or announcement about the event taking place. It relied on being in the right place at the right time, with the right circumstances and just the right people around. Kind of like when the planets all line up together.

It was late afternoon, and a light rain was falling, although the sun peeked through every once in a while. I was at Curves exercising, and one of the women had just finished her workout and was walking out the door. She came back in a moment later and said, "Hey, there's a double rainbow!"

Hopping off my exercise machine, I ran outside to look. One rainbow was bright and intense, and looked so solid you could imagine exactly where both sides touched down to earth. The other rainbow was above the first one—and yes, I realize that means it was "somewhere over the rainbow"—but it was faint, gentle, and fading quickly. Still, it was there.

I ran back inside to get my phone/camera, and came back out clicking away. I moved to different areas of the parking lot and sidewalk to get shots from various angles, and that's when I saw something else that was bright and stunning. It had nothing to do with the rainbow, however, and it had been there all along, although I hadn't really noticed it. It was the spire of the old church across the street, surrounded by a sea of red, orange, and gold as the leaves on the tree next to it waved about in all their autumn glory. One end of the rainbow dropped down behind the church.

It took my breath away.

It also reminded me that it's not always the big, grand, much-heralded events—or the ones we plan for and look forward to the most—that give us the greatest pleasures in life. Often, it's the small, quiet ones that just show up when we least expect them. All we need to do is pay attention.

It's not always the big, grand events—or the ones we plan for and look forward to the most—that give us the greatest pleasures in life. Often, it's the small, quiet ones that just show up when we least expect them.

Find Another Nugget: Unusual cloud formations, the fall colors, a gentle snowfall, or a torrential rain—take time to notice a seasonal or situational aspect of nature that you've stopped paying attention to and now take for granted. Remind yourself of the natural beauty that is all around you, or can be found in your environment. Spend a few minutes just noticing and watching it.

Chapter 29 - April 23, 2015

Oops!

We had friends over for dinner last weekend, and our meal included cheesecake for dessert. It was from a recipe I've had for a long time, although I've never actually made it before. It was labor-intensive and time-consuming, with a lot of prep work required and some tricky steps along the way. At one point, things didn't look the way they were supposed to, and I started worrying that instead of cheesecake, we'd be eating cheesecake soup for dessert. But it turned out fine, and was delicious.

The meal also included a side dish that's a family favorite. I make it fairly often, and don't need to look at the recipe anymore. It has only four ingredients, and is put together at the last minute. I was in the middle of preparing it, a half-hour before dinner, when I realized I didn't have one of the ingredients I needed. It was something I always have on hand—like salt and pepper, or sugar and flour—but somehow I had run out of it. It was more of a topping than a main ingredient, so I didn't have to scrap the entire dish or make a last-minute run to the grocery store. But the dish wasn't quite as good without it, and I was kicking myself for my slip-up.

There's a lesson in here somewhere.

Actually, there are several, and they have nothing to do with food. One is about paying attention to things we often take for granted, and not neglecting the minor details. Another is that the ordinary, everyday aspects of our lives are every bit as important—if not more so—than the big, special-occasion ones.

The main lesson, though, is about not losing sight of the big picture, or of what's most important in our lives. Our dinner last weekend wasn't really about the food. It was about spending time with people we care about and whose company we enjoy. It didn't matter to them that the side dish I served wasn't exactly right, or that we almost ended up with a soggy cheesecake for dessert—which would have given us something to laugh about at future get-togethers—or with no dessert at all. Even if we had just ordered a pizza, or had only snacks and drinks, we still would have enjoyed ourselves.

What struck me the most last weekend was how much I enjoy taking the time and making the effort to put together something special for special people. I also realized that the people who are most special to me don't expect or care about things being perfect, or perfectly prepared. Our best friends are the ones with whom we can share our "oops" stories and experiences. They help us laugh at our mistakes instead of stressing out over them. They enjoy and appreciate what we do, and they keep us from being too hard on ourselves when we mess up.

They also help us remember that humble pie isn't nearly as tasty as cheesecake.

 We should never lose sight of the big picture—what's most important in our lives.

Find Another Nugget: When you make a mistake, or when something goes wrong in your life, take a few steps back so that instead of focusing on the details, you can remember the bigger picture: What is it you were trying to accomplish? Why? What was your ultimate goal, and why is it important to you? Can you still get there from where you are now? Answering these questions can help you keep things in perspective so that mistakes and mishaps don't stop you in your tracks or keep you from reaching your goals and enjoying your achievements.

Chapter 30 - July 23, 2015

All Fired Up

This is going to sound like something I totally made up, but I swear I'm telling it exactly as it happened—in a dream I had a few nights ago. Actually, it was early morning, since my alarm went off and woke me up before the dream was finished. I'm glad it did, because it kept the dream fresh and vivid enough for me to write it all down before it drifted away.

In the dream, I was attending a meeting of a women's networking group. It was one I'd never been to before, and I didn't really know anyone there. One of the women started talking about being fired up, and it seemed to be an inside joke. Everyone else knew what she was talking about except me. So she explained.

The woman had worked for a very small company that was going through hard times. Other people had been getting laid off at regular intervals, but she had managed to hold on to her job, in part because the woman she worked for was the owner of the company. They worked very well together, and had also developed a strong professional friendship. Hearing this woman talk, I could easily tell how much loyalty, respect, and appreciation they felt toward each other.

Eventually, however, her time came. Her boss called her in to her office and told her she had to let her go, but she gave her such enthusiastic encouragement and such powerful praise—as well as glowing references—that the woman felt as though she'd been promoted rather than fired.

"I feel like I got fired up," the woman told me in the dream. "And I've been fired up ever since."

Still dreaming, I said to the woman, "This is exactly the kind of thing I like to write about in my column. May I?"

She hesitated before answering. Understandably, since we didn't really know each other, and she wasn't familiar with my writing. So I assured her—as I do in real life when I'm planning to write about what other people said or did—that I would protect her privacy, and there would be nothing nasty or negative in anything I wrote. Before I could say anything else, my alarm clock went off and woke me up, which was good in another way as it meant I didn't need to get the woman's permission or approval before writing about her.

I could refer to this whole incident as "living in a dream world," but wouldn't that indeed be a great place to be? Just imagine a world where mutual loyalty, respect, and appreciation were the norm, not the exception. And not just between bosses and their employees, but among us all.

I can't change how other people think or act, but I can start by working on the loyalty, respect, and appreciation I show to others. I'm willing to bet it will have a positive ripple effect. I hope so. This may be an idea I dreamed up while I was sound asleep, but now, wide awake, I'm pretty fired up about it.

 Imagine a world where mutual loyalty, respect, and appreciation are the norm, not the exception.

Find Another Nugget: If there's a relationship, personal or professional, in which you and the other person don't have very positive feelings toward each other, take a few minutes now to think about what it would take to change that. Have an imaginary conversation, write your own ending, and see what starts happening in your life. You may just find yourself getting fired up in ways you've never imagined, ways that take you beyond your wildest dreams.

Nuggets

Here's a list of the nuggets mined from the columns in this book:

1. There's no place like home. But the view is different now, because we see things differently as adults than we did as children, and because the world has changed so much since then.

2. To achieve success in anything, you need to push, pull, and stretch. Work a little harder, and reach a little farther, but don't do anything that hurts.

3. It's comforting and heartwarming to be told, out loud, that we are valued and appreciated, and to hear in specific detail the positive traits others see in us.

4. Trust feels good, no matter which end of the deal you're on.

5. Take the time to sit quietly and listen to the sounds of silence, and you'll hear more than you've ever heard before.

6. When many hands are working together, they don't just lighten the load, they lighten the mood.

7. Don't miss out on a golden opportunity just because there are other things you need to do. Some opportunities do, indeed, knock only once.

8. Everyone is as valuable as everyone else. Some have more prominent roles, but it takes everyone—working side by side and holding on to each other—to put the picture together the way it's supposed to be.

9. Never get so caught up in thinking about life's dangers that it keeps you from enjoying life's many delights.

10. It feels good to let others know we notice and appreciate their kindness, and then to feel their appreciation in return.

11. If you believe that failure is not an option, then it isn't.

12. Knowing about someone else's good fortune, and being happy about it, can feel pretty good for us, too.

13. Be courteous and attentive to other drivers out on the road, and remember that such courtesy works both ways.

14. It's a gift to see beauty in everyday things. Treasure this!

15. Persistence and determination are traits that people admire, and that are most likely to bring us success, accomplishment, and personal satisfaction.

16. We can get knowledge and education from books, but we get wisdom and experience from people.

17. Bad habits are easy to make and difficult to break, while the opposite is true for good habits. So when we find some tricks and tools that help us make and maintain the good ones, we should hang on to them.

18. There's comfort in having something we recognize, something we can count on, something familiar.

19. Whenever you help someone else, you end up helping yourself even more.

20. The more we pare down in any area of our lives, the more we'll be able to use and enjoy whatever is left.

21. It is our daily practices that determine whether or not we'll reach our goals, complete our plans, and achieve our dreams. When our daily practices are enjoyable in and of themselves, we are much more likely to continue doing them.

22. Finishing something does not mean "The End." It usually means the beginning.

23. Ask yourself these two questions: Am I passionate about what I'm doing? Do I genuinely care about the people I am working with? Answering "Yes" to both can determine or improve your chances for success.

24. There are many treasures to be found in our everyday lives—as long as we're paying attention, are willing to explore, and are ready to receive them.

25. Sometimes it's not the good things that happen to us, but rather the bad things, that help us the most.

26. The more people who are in harmony with each other, the better we'll all be.

27. Our memories, not our possessions, are our greatest treasures.

28. It's not always the big, grand events—or the ones we plan for and look forward to the most—that give us the greatest pleasures in life. Often, it's the small, quiet ones that just show up when we least expect them.

29. We should never lose sight of the big picture— what's most important in our lives.

30. Imagine a world where mutual loyalty, respect, and appreciation are the norm, not the exception.

Acknowledgments

The list of people I want to thank for their help in producing this book could easily be longer than the book itself. I'll try to stop before I get that far, and hope that those I don't name directly will still know how grateful I am for their help and input.

Family always comes first, and I owe much of who, what, and where I am to my husband Steve, son Kurt, and daughter Robin, as well as to Mom, Dad, and sisters Kathy, Barb, and Chris. Thank you for your love, support, and encouragement that have been with me every day of my life. An extra thank you to Robin, who has given me much artistic and creative advice, and to other family members whose interest and support I cherish.

Thank you to my *Chanhassen Villager* family, especially editor Dick Crawford and features reporter Unsie Zuege, who is now also a treasured friend, and to my "Curves" family, especially Melissa Olson, who always shines a spotlight on my weekly columns.

Thank you, Connie Anderson, for your editing and expertise, and to all the women of WOW, especially WOW2, my "primary residence" in the Women of Words family. Your talent and creativity are exceeded only by your generosity of spirit and the genuine pleasure we all get from helping and seeing each other succeed. A special thank you to Michelle Gardner for her gift of the perfect subtitle, which had been eluding me for months, to Nancy Gahl and Julie Siekkenan for their brilliant artistic input, and to Diane Keyes for editing and tightening a key area of the book.

I am extremely grateful to Dara Beevas of Wise Ink for her wise counsel, and to Ann Aubitz of FuzionPress for her expertise, guidance, and skills that turned my humble manuscript into a beautiful book. I am also grateful to Lorna Landvik, Dana LaMon, and Stephen Shaner for their gracious and generous words in support of the book.

Thank you to Toastmasters International, and especially my home club of Marsh Winds. The words we speak are as important as the words we write, and you have helped me polish them all till they shine.

The Master Track program at The Loft in Minneapolis taught me to dig deeper into my life and my stories in ways that improved my writing immensely. Thank you to my advisor and mentor Elizabeth Jarrett Andrew, to Cheri Register, and to Kathy Ogle, Maggie O'Connor, and Unsie Zuege, who forged new paths with me in our voyage through Creative Nonfiction. Thanks also to Therese Zink, who joined us later for part of that journey.

Jeannette Potter, your interest and encouragement in my writing, as well as the love of reading that we share, have always been a joy, and I am very grateful to you. I also want to thank Christy Snede, Sandy Ryan, and Karen Bennett for always being in my corner with love, support, and enthusiasm as we worked on our dreams and goals. This certainly is one of them! And TiCo, I can't begin to thank you enough for all the creativity and delight you have added to my life and my writing.

This book has been on my mind and in my plans for a long time, and it was Bob Voss who gave me exactly what I needed to really get it off the ground. Thank you, Bob!

Other people helped me with nudges and shoves whenever I got stuck somewhere or had trouble starting up again. I am especially grateful to Mary Jo Sherwood, Glen Lewerenz, Tabitha Kyambadde, and Nikki Abramson for their support and suggestions, and to Rena Musyt, whose wisdom, insights, friendship, and encouragement have always been an inspiration to me.

The content of each column is the same as when it was first published in the *Chanhassen Villager*. However, some minor editing was necessary in the transition from column to book. I am extremely grateful to the *Villager*, not only for allowing me to share my voice and viewpoints in the paper every week, but for granting permission to reprint the columns in this collection.

I will always be indebted to those who have inspired or been a part of the columns I've written, and who have taught me the lessons that were buried inside each experience. I am equally grateful for everyone who has read and enjoyed my columns over the years. I hope you will continue to find the buried treasure that is around all of us, everywhere, in our day-to-day lives.

About the Author

Betty Liedtke is an award-winning columnist, Certified Dream Coach™, and the Founder/CEO of Find Your Buried Treasure™. Her mission in life is helping people to see the gifts, skills, strengths, and talents they don't even realize they have, and inspiring them to use these gifts to change their lives and the world.

Photo by Dani Werner

A survivor of cancer and severe heart damage following chemotherapy, Betty always looks at the bright side of any situation or experience, even when she has to dig to find it. In addition to her work in the United States, Betty travels regularly to Uganda, where she helps students, teachers, and church and business leaders to find the buried treasure in their own lives.

Betty and her husband live in Minnesota, where they raised their two children.

To contact Betty, or for more information about her work, visit her website at
www.findyourburiedtreasure.com